How to X your ex

A GUIDE TO GETTING PAST UNHEALTHY RELATIONSHIPS

ASHLEIGH GUICE

ISBN-13: 978-1541326989

ISBN-10: 1541326989

Cover and interior typesetting by Vanessa Mendozzi

Cover images purchased under license Shutterstock.com

First Edition First Printing

Contents

Why this book?

Let's be honest, break ups suck. Going through a break up can be hard and getting over your ex can be even harder. Think about it, how many times have you had a breakup that you really needed to get past? Or a relationship where you genuinely wanted it to work but it crashed and burned? Well I myself lost count. I feel like I've had more break ups than relationships. Nevertheless, I knew that there was a lesson to every relationship I went through but it wasn't until later in my journey that I learned that a person could master the art of moving on.

I have found that there are healthy ways to moving past old relationships. There is no perfect way to heal your heart once it has been broken but there are steps that a person can take to help ease the heartache.

I've dated so many men and went through so many break ups that I wouldn't want anyone, male or female, to have to take any more time getting over someone than necessary. If I knew in the beginning the proper way to move on, I could have saved so much energy and most of all TIME. If you actually calculate how much time you lose by dwelling on your past, then you will understand why it is so important to move on as quickly as possible.

I can recall my breakup with my first real love. He and I went to high school together, and he graduated one year before me. I had the biggest crush on him, and I knew he would never date a senior in high school since he was an alumnus. Well, I couldn't have been more wrong, because what started as a small flirtation soon became a full-blown romance. (Yeah, I know I was only seventeen, but this was my first love, so I felt like Julia Roberts in *Pretty Woman*—minus the hooker angle, of course. He and I were attached at the hip. We would see each other every single day. Even if it was just a five-minute hug and kiss, we had to do it because we couldn't miss a day without seeing each other. I even spent time with his grandmother and aunts. I just knew this love would last a lifetime. Well boys will be boys and I was truly heartbroken when I found out my first love was cheating on me. Oh, it hurt. Badly. I can still remember that feeling, like a bus had just hit me. I hurt everywhere. My emotional agony had transformed into physical pain.

Being that this was my first breakup, I had no clue how to heal my heart or even lessen the pain I was feeling emotionally, mentally, and even physically. The first thing I did was text him to tell him it was over and I knew everything. I told him not to call, text, or even breathe my air. I basically told him to forget I existed. I then avoided all his calls and texts for the next three months. During this time, I plotted out all the evil things I could do to get revenge, like egg his car or teepee his house or physically beat him up. After three months of anger, I finally spoke to him and told him how much I hated him and wished he didn't have limbs. Forgiveness wasn't really my forte. I felt that hurting him like he had hurt me was better, so me being evil to him was the trick.

I even thought that if I dated someone else, it would

make me feel better and also make him jealous. Killing two birds with one stone is what I thought I was doing. Well, all these efforts were a huge and utter failure because, after two years of dating other people, I woke up one day realizing that I had never actually gotten over my first love. I was still holding on to what he had done to me and I noticed how his actions and my anger shaped my dating life tremendously. It took a number of failed attempts at dating for me to develop the wisdom to see that I had never taken the time to heal after my first love broke my heart.

Now fast forward a few years to a more recent break up. This is where I began to see that finding healthy ways to X your ex really does work for your best interest.

This young man and I had known each other for about a year, but we didn't start off seriously. When we initially dated, he wasn't ready to get serious because he was focused on his career. We remained friends, and one day after we'd begun seeing each other more often, we decided to try dating. It was a great relationship. We saw each other at least four times a week and we conversed daily. We talked about everything; our history and hopes for the future. We were so compatible and we both enjoyed spending time with one another. To me, everything was perfect. One day we decided to take our first road trip. We went white water rafting, and we bonded quite nicely. Well, at the close of that very weekend he told me we needed to talk, and I knew this was the end of our relationship. It caught me completely off guard because we were in the middle of honeymoon stage. Who gets dumped in honeymoon stage? Me, that's who! He said that we had a great weekend together but he wasn't ready for a relationship…again.

Of course, I was hurt but the way I handled this breakup was way different from that first one. I had learned that I went through different phases after each breakup, and how I handled those phases would determine how quickly my heart would heal.

These phases include:

PHASE 1

Let It Out... I cried for about a week straight. I had to. I had to cry it all out because me holding onto my emotions and trying to act tough did nothing for me. I let it out so I could forgive him and move on.

PHASE 2

This is NOT a Contact Sport, Cut it Out... I had to force myself NOT to contact him, because I knew I was still vulnerable and that contacting him would only take me back to phase one.

PHASE 3

Rebounds are Only Good in Basketball... I decided not to date anyone to avoid falling into a rebound relationship. Instead, I wanted to use healthy distractions to get my mind off my disappointment. You never want to open a new door if you haven't closed the previous one.

PHASE 4

The Closure Trap... I focused on getting over him alone, understanding that I did not need closure from him in order to move on.

PHASE 5

Give It to Your God... I prayed each and every day. I needed strength and encouragement to get me through not just this break up but how I felt about myself. Most situations can't be handled in life without some spiritual presence.

PHASE 6

Perception is Reality... If you dwell on all the things that made you happy during the relationship when you initially break up, you will just make yourself miserable.

PHASE 7

Fighting Lonely... I was finally feeling great and could see the light, but I had to remain strong and fight loneliness to avoid any relapse.

PHASE 8

Self Reflection... After my tears had dried and I was in a better place, I had to self-reflect on the lesson learned from this relationship. I like to believe that everything happens for a reason and we must pull a life lesson from every situation we go through, be it big or small.

Every person is different and behaves differently. I know that. This is not a book for people looking for the easy way out or a quick fix. There are times where these phases will feel uncomfortable and you might feel like quitting but don't. You can do it! This book is designed to change your way of thinking about breakups and to mend those heartaches of the past and present so that you can have a healthy and happy future as you move on from your ex. There's no way of telling how long the healing process will take. However, I know that if you adhere to these phases honestly and correctly it will mend those heartaches that you never thought you would get past. Experience has been my greatest teacher and I will reveal my personal stories throughout this book to help you understand each phase. I along with several other close friends can tell you that this process works.

Now let me teach you how to X your ex.

PHASE 1

Let it Out

In 2013, I rekindled an old flame with someone I thought was my knight in shining armor. When we originally met, I just knew he was my Will Smith and I his Jada Pinkett. Well, it didn't quite work out that way. We met through a mutual friend from college during our freshman year. We hung out a few times but it just wasn't in the stars for us at that moment. He was an athlete and hadn't gotten through his 'playa' stage yet. For those of you who don't know what a 'playa' stage is, that is when a man feels he needs to pursue every woman he can so he won't miss out on anything. One woman is not enough in 'playa' stage; he has to have them all. After realizing this,

I decided to remove myself from the equation and let him be a 'playa'. I never thought we would speak again, but I was pleasantly surprised to bump into him six years later.

I was at a local lounge in Atlanta when he spotted me on the dancefloor. I was heading toward the exit when he stopped me. I was shocked but happy to see him. He told me he'd be in town for a few days and would love to do lunch. I agreed and gave him my number. I actually had no intention of having lunch with him because I remembered the kind of guy he was. At age 24, I didn't have time to be dealing with a 'playa'. Well, he never contacted me, so I didn't have to tell him no. This also further proved my point that he was still the same guy I met in college.

To my surprise, six months later he contacted me. He sent me a text asking if I could use my connections to help find a good deal for a birthday party. At the time I was working at an upscale lounge. I knew that booking this party was a good business opportunity for me so I agreed. I handled the booking, and everything went well.

The night of the party, I made sure to look flawless because I knew I would see him. I guess I had some sort of semi-buried feelings for him to go out of my way to get dolled up, but I didn't want him see me at less than perfect.

Nearing the end of the party, he approached me thanking me for putting everything together. Looking at him, he seemed to be way calmer than the college boy I had met six years prior. He was well dressed and very cool. While his friends were drunk and acting wild, he remained sober and in control. This behavior suggested that maybe he had changed from the boy I cut ties with in college; maybe he was more of a man than I'd previously thought.

After the party, he once again asked if I wanted to do lunch. This time, I was up for it…and this time I *did* hear from him. We had a great time. He told me that he worked in North Dakota but had a home in Atlanta. He even apologized for how he acted when we initially met. He said he was indeed in 'playa' stage and regretted losing me. He said all the right things, and the lunch ended with him asking if we could try again. I hesitated somewhat because of the past, but I could really see that he wasn't the same person. I told him I would think about it, already knowing I would say yes but wanting to make him sweat. I later called him and said I'd like to give it a try.

Initially, it was awesome! The distance was tough because he was in North Dakota for months at a time but we made it work. We Facetimed at least four nights a week and talked all day long by text. He would spoil me with presents and send me flowers for no reason. Three months after our lunch date, he bought me a ticket to visit him in North Dakota. The trip was amazing, and I felt we were perfect for one another. Little did I know this marked the end of our relationship.

After I returned to Atlanta, he became very distant. The Facetime calls stopped, and we went from talking all day to me literally having to stalk him to get him on the phone. I felt so hurt, because I didn't understand what had gone wrong. I asked him if everything was okay, and he responded with the infamous "I'm just busy" line. The final straw for me was when he flew to Atlanta and made no effort to see me. I was done. This is a guy who had sold me major dreams of happiness. He would constantly say things like, "This is our year," and "Don't be afraid to fall for me because I'll always be here." He introduced me to friends and family, and took me to church with his mom. I was all in because I thought he was all in, too. Especially because he pursued me for a second chance and I had given him one. Although I had put all of my eggs in his basket, I refused to be anyone's fool, so I had to leave him alone.

Once we broke up, I pretended everything was okay and started to go on dates and party a lot. I never sat down to think about the pain because I was too busy ignoring it. I was one month into the "healing" process when I came across an old picture of us in my phone. When I saw the picture, I just stared at it and tears filled my eyes instantly. I threw my phone and just cried for an hour straight. A month had gone by and I hadn't stopped to react to the pain. I had been holding it all in. I wasted a month running from the pain when I should have been releasing it.

When going through any emotional conflict in life, you always want to begin by releasing all of your pent-up feelings. In this situation, I cried for a while. I sat down and really thought about what he had done, determined to get it out. Everyone is different when it comes to how they release pain, but you have to do it. The worst thing you can do is hold it in the way I did, still extremely angry a month later, as if it had happened yesterday.

A really good way to relieve some of that anger and really understand every emotion you're going through is something I call 'Letter to My Ex'. This is basically the act of putting down on paper every single thing you want to say to your ex. I don't care if you're reluctant to say it or if you have too much pride; write it down in this letter. This is not for your ex to see—you're never going to send it—it is for you to let all those emotions out so you can realize what really happened and why you truly need to move on. Here is an example of a letter I wrote:

Dear _____, (Put your ex's name here? Try it.)

It kills me how men can come into your life, fuck it up, then vanish, leaving you to figure out where it all went wrong. How dare you?! Here I was minding my own business, living my sweet life and here you come asking me for a second chance. If you weren't ready to give your all then why interrupt the greatness I had going on? What's crazy is, I don't even give second chances but I gave you one because I thought you deserved it. HA! The only thing you deserve is to be slapped upside that weird shaped head of yours. I can still remember our lunch date when you delivered a bunch of sugar coated lies like "This is our year" and "I would never hurt you". Well guess what; YOU HURT ME!

When I came to visit you in North Dakota, everything was awesome. I met your married friends and they were even trying to convince me to move there. I thought we reached another level of our relationship but that was a huge misconception. When I got home, we barely talked. I would text you back to back and wouldn't get a reply for hours. You ignored every single FaceTime call just to say you were busy working extra shifts. I told myself to let it go because I knew you would be in Atlanta in a few weeks. When you came here, you treated me like a second-hand groupie. Out of three days, I saw you a total of five hours. How the hell are you going to tell me you're coming to Atlanta to see me and only give me five freaking hours of your time?

Oh and let's not forget the hotel incident. I booked us one of the nicest hotels in the city for a romantic evening. I waited hours for you just to get a text saying you can't make it right before midnight. Wow...I can't believe you did that to me and I still came to church with you and your mother on that Sunday hoping it could salvage the remnants of our relationship. Why would you introduce me to your mom knowing you were about to leave me? There is a special place in hell for men like you.

It hurts so much because I let my guard down. I went against my "no second chances" rule and I let you in. I had no defense up with you and you took advantage of that. What I can't understand is why a huge part of me blames myself for part of this. I knew you were a 'playa' in your past so why would I believe you? I knew what you were capable of but I told myself I had to let go of that past in order to give us a try. See men always complain that women can't let go of the past but that's a lie. I let go for you! But how do you repay me? You throw me away like last week's leftovers. See this is the type of bull that makes those bitter black women everyone likes to talk about. Men come into our lives with horrible intentions and when they break our hearts we have to put the pieces back together. No wonder why so many black women have bitchy attitudes and emotional walls as big as the Wall of China. But I won't give you that power. I will NOT allow you to steal joy from me any longer. You had your chance and I know that karma is a pretty little bitch and she will come back around. As for me, the best revenge is living well and that is exactly what I am going to do. So damn you and that cold ass North Dakota because this is goodbye!

In those words I let out all my vulnerable feelings. He never read that letter because it was never meant for him to see it. I wrote it to let it out. Every time I found myself missing him I'd read that letter to remind myself of why I was letting go. I no longer wanted to dwell on the false hope that we could possibly get back together. To tell you the truth, that is the hardest part of letting go. Once you give up on the false hope that one day you'll wake up and that person will be totally in love with you and it will all work out, then you can easily walk away. This letter will help you let go of that fantasy. It will help you see that you are walking away for a good reason and that you don't need to look back because you need to heal yourself.

Although you should definitely not send your "Letter to My Ex", it doesn't mean that you cannot express how you feel to your ex. Another form of expressing your anger is to simply let that individual know what they have done. This is very difficult and must be handled delicately. Now, I'm not telling you to go bang on their door right now and tell them how you feel. I'm talking about a more tactical method. If you are able to set up a meeting with your ex and feel you're strong enough to tell them how you feel face to face, go for it. If you feel you're not strong enough, then write your ex an email or text, but you want to express relevant factors that will help you heal. What I mean by that is get to the meat of the subject. You just want him or her to know "You hurt me, this is the reason I feel you hurt me, and this is why I am moving on." Write down what you want to say so you don't forget in the heat of the moment. These conversations are to be had once you have gotten rid of all that initial emotion. The last thing you want to do is call your ex when you just finished a bottle of wine and Drake is playing in the background. Your emotions will lead and logic will go out of the window. You want to have a logical, well-thought-out conversation.

If this person is willing to talk, then listen but never expect anything. Having high expectations about how your ex will respond will almost certainly leave you very disappointed. They may not be remorseful, they may be very nonchalant showing they don't care, or they may not say anything at all. Expect the worst in order to be prepared. But the objective of this step is not to receive a response, it is for you to put everything on the table and release every emotion in your heart. Once your emotions are on the table, you can move toward forgiveness.

The September 2014 issue of *Psychology Today* featured an article written by Rubin Khoddam entitled 'The Psychology of Forgiveness.' In this article, the author explains that "Forgiveness is not saying you accept the person who wronged you. Instead, forgiveness is choosing to accept what happened as it happened rather than what could or should have happened." Understanding that we can't change what happened but can learn to accept it allows us to move forward without the baggage of the past weighing us down. Most individuals get the idea of forgiveness confused. They think forgiveness is for the benefit of the offender when it is really for the person who's been offended. There are so many people holding on to their pasts and have yet to forgive someone for hurting them, and it is ruining their lives. Their current relationships are suffering because they keep making others pay for what someone else did to them in the past. Well, guess what? That person you hate so much is sleeping just fine and hasn't thought about you in years. They are living a happy life while you're holding on to all your anger, which results in your constantly thinking of them. This is why forgiveness is meant for the victim. When you forgive, life is so much more peaceful. That ex you can't stand is no longer on your mind, in your dreams, or coming up in your conversations five years later. Burdens are now lifted off your shoulders and you can now move on with a happy heart. Forgiveness does not mean you agree with their actions or how they treated you. Forgiveness also does not mean you should take that person back or be their friend. It simply means that your feelings toward them have changed and you can now wish them well from a distance.

I know you may be thinking, "I can't do that; they broke my heart. I won't forgive them, they don't deserve it." Never allow pride to get in the way of your healing process. I ran from my emotions and did not want my ex to know how much he had hurt me because I felt it would make me sound desperate and weak. This was way too much for my ego. The biggest part about this step is understanding that it has nothing to do with the offender but has everything to do with the offended: you.

Telling someone how you feel when he or she hurt

you only transfers ownership. Most of the time we blame ourselves for the failure of relationships when it is truly not our fault. (I am not referring to cheaters, because if you cheated, it was your fault and this part isn't for you.) It also makes your heart so much lighter because really, all you wanted was for someone to hear you. You just want to say exactly how they made you feel because if you don't, it can eat you up inside. So stop being so hard and guarded and let your heart speak for once because it needs to.

If you continue to hold it in, not only does it prolong your healing process; it just starts to build up and will eventually erupt. I found myself taking it out on my friends and family when they didn't deserve it. It was all displaced anger because I didn't let it out to begin with. You have to release it, no matter what. Until you have done this, you can never move on to the next step. Remember to let it all out and do not let pride get in your way.

"Proud people breed sad sorrows for themselves."

\- Emily Brontë

PHASE 2

This is Not a Contact Sport, Cut It Out

Amongst my friends I am known as "Queen Cut Them Off". If you do not know what "cut them off" means, it's pretty straightforward. It simply means cutting ties with someone and having absolutely no contact with that person. No texting, no emailing, no social media stalking, and no breathing their air; *no contact*. I gained this title by my ability to delete a person's number and block them as soon as it becomes apparent they're up to no good. I know you're thinking, "What does this have to do with getting past an ex?" Well, I am here to tell you that it has *everything* to do with it. When I decided to stop all contact with those who had wronged me, I did it initially because

I was angry. I did not realize that it was actually helping me to heal and move past them as well. This phase will explain how having no contact can be your saving grace when trying to X your ex.

Once you get past your initial uncontrollable emotion and get back to logic, this step must go into effect immediately. After you've cried it out and let your ex know how you feel, there is nothing left to say so you will say nothing to them. No contact is the goal. No texting. No calling. No Instagram stalking. No Facebook messaging. No emailing. No direct mailing. NO CONTACT. They shouldn't have a way to contact you, either, so block them. Block them from your phone, Facebook, Instagram, email, and even your neighborhood if you have to. NO CONTACT.

This sounds harsh, I know, but there is a method to the madness. If you continue to talk to your ex or let them have the power to reach out to you any time they want, it will delay your healing process. Think of it as rehab. If a recovering drug addict has access to drugs or drugs have access to them at any given time, how well do you think their treatment would go? Horribly! If you are truly committed to getting over someone, you should not want to contact him or her anyway. You are trying to completely close this door, not leave it cracked so your ex can just walk back in.

Now, let's break this down by explaining the 'why' behind it all. Let's talk more about Mr. North Dakota. After getting my anger out and realizing that he and I would never work, I finally stopped thinking about him every day. It went down to me having thoughts of him twice a week instead of twice a day, which was great for me. Now, I had already deleted his number and hadn't spoken to him in weeks, but he still had access to me. One day about two months into no contact, I was watching television and received a text message. Lo and behold, it was him and, oh, did that piss me off. The message read:

"I am in town and I would like to see you so we can talk."

WHAT?! So *now* you want to talk?! My stomach curled into knots, my head got warm and my face turned red all over. I was furious.

So many things went through my head, and I got mad all over again. How dare he text me asking to see me when I begged to see him for months and he always had an excuse? How dare he even think he can ask me that question, like we're on good terms? Oh, if I had a train I would have run him over right then and there. All these thoughts ran through my head, but the only thing my thumb could type was:

> "No, I am not ready to see you, but enjoy your trip."

I wanted to say so many things, but nothing mattered, because at that moment my peace was interrupted and it took my healing from 20% back to 5%. Although I told him I didn't want to see him, I stalked his Instagram that entire weekend. I got mad at every picture posted because he was having so much fun. I wanted him to be miserable like he had made me. To make matters worse, several pictures showed him with another young lady. So not only was he having fun, he was having fun with a new woman! My blood was boiling, but I had only myself to blame because I left that door cracked and he did what most exes do—he walked right back in.

Now can you see how holding on to that contact can have a ripple effect? If he had already been blocked, then he would have had no way to contact me. And if he had not contacted me, I never would have looked at his Instagram and seen that he had a new chick. All these factors served to put me right back at square one and ruined all my previous progress. That is why breaking up is not a contact sport, because contact just ruins growth.

Many of you are reading this and figuring out how to adjust this to fit your current situation. Thoughts like *"There's no way I can go without contacting my ex at all,"* are flooding your mind. Well, if this doesn't sound like something you can do, then you may want to ask yourself if you are really ready to X your ex. If you are really ready, then you would be willing to commit to a task you have never attempted, no matter how uncomfortable. When you commit 50%, then your results will be

50%. For those who think adjusting the no-contact phase to fit what you're comfortable with will yield the same results, let me give you an example of what will most likely happen.

I have a male friend who had been with his girlfriend for almost two years. They were perfect the first year, but after that, something went wrong and they never quite got back on track. For the past year, he has called me every other week telling me how toxic their relationship had become and how he wanted to leave but he didn't know what to do. I gave him the same advice I just gave you, but he only took part of the advice. His biggest issue was that he couldn't go without contacting her and he refused to block her from contacting him. Every time he called me saying that she lied to him or that he couldn't do this anymore I told him, "Stop calling her and stop allowing her to call you." He said okay, hung up the phone, then two weeks later he called me back saying the same exact thing and the cycle continued.

Does this sound like your current reality? Do you feel like every time you think you're ready to move past your ex they just pull you right back in? Well, let me tell you a secret. It isn't that they're pulling you back in; it's that mentally, you never really left in the first place. You can't keep doing the same thing and expecting different results. In order to remove your ex from your life, mentally and spiritually as well as physically, you have to do something different and be uncomfortable. You can't pick and choose what advice fits you and then wonder why it isn't working. If you're tired of going in circles and feel really ready to break away this time, you need to commit to every single step and not select what is comfortable. Change is not, has never been, and never will be comfortable.

If my male friend was really ready to be over his ex, then he would have stopped all contact. He thought that continuing contact would've allowed him to ease out of the relationship slowly rather than going cold turkey. Let's go back to the drug addict example. If a crack addict decided they wanted to quit so they stopped smoking crack twice a day and went down to once a day, how long will it take before they stopped using drugs completely? Never! Look at your ex like that drug. You can't tell yourself, "I want to quit," then turn around and dip and dab occasionally. No, no, no…you need to go cold turkey.

NO CONTACT. If you think taking shortcuts will help you X your ex, then you'll be just like my friend, calling a confidante every two weeks with the same exact issue. Commit to the process with no shortcuts and stop the cycle.

This phase is probably the most uncomfortable and difficult of all, but it is also the most important. I know it's hard to no longer have contact with someone you're probably used to talking to every single day, possibly more than once per day, but you must remember that with growth there will always be some form of discomfort. Removing someone from your life will always be painful. The pain will not last long if you take the proper steps to stop it now. When you have a major injury, the first thing you do is go to the doctor and they give you the proper steps of healing. These steps are painful, but you do them because you want to heal properly. When you take shortcuts you can potentially cause more pain, which makes the healing process longer. The same goes for healing your heart. If you are truly serious about getting over your ex, then you will commit to this step and you will not take any shortcuts. That means you will not reach out to them, nor will you give them access to reach out to you. Healing your heart is not a contact sport, so cut it out.

"When the past calls, let it go to voicemail. It has nothing to say."

\- Mandy Hale

PHASE 3

Rebounds are Only Good in Basketball

Have you ever heard the expression "The best way to get over someone is to get under someone new"? It is basically saying that in order to get past a breakup you must move on to someone new. This is an absolutely horrible idea. At some point in life you might have done this and you might have had a bit of temporary success but trust me, this is a horrible way to move on. When this step is taken, it creates something we like to call a rebound. We all know that a rebound is someone you settle for when the person you really wanted didn't work out. It doesn't sound too good when you actually think about it.

Still not convinced that a rebound is a bad idea? Look at it this way, have you ever fallen and gotten a cut or a scrape and you started to bleed? The first thing you thought to do was put a Band-Aid on it. Once this Band-Aid was applied, your wound was healed, right? Wrong! Look at a rebound like that Band-Aid. You were hurt, so you're looking for a quick fix to make your scar feel better, but underneath the surface you're still bleeding and you still must fully heal.

I have had a number of rebounds in life, so I am witness to the damage. When I went out with these men, I was only looking for a temporary fix to my situation. I just wanted to feel better. I wanted someone to hold me and kiss me, wanted to feel like everything would be okay. Yes, I received that temporary high from these situations that I was looking for. But it was only temporary, and in the long run it actually did more damage.

Coming out of an emotional situation, you're only thinking about yourself. You aren't really aware of someone else's emotion because you're too busy trying to control your own. Shortly after my breakup with Mr. North Dakota, I began dating a new guy. At first, it was just relaxing and fun. He would take me out on dates and we would laugh together. We started to spend a lot of time together, and I felt it was harmless because I hadn't been thinking about North Dakota anymore. It seemed innocent, and I was just going with the flow. What I didn't stop to think about was how the other person in the rebound relationship felt.

This guy was great. Caring, supportive, great to talk to, and he even had a good sense of humor. He would have been a great mate if I met him at another time. I thought we were just dating and having fun to make me feel better. What I failed to realize was that this was real for him and he had started to develop feelings for me. I started to feel better and realized I no longer needed him because he had served his purpose. By the time I realized this, he wanted all of me, which I couldn't give because I wasn't taking our relationship seriously. He was only there to distract me from dealing with my break up. So now not only was I still not fully over North Dakota, but I had hurt someone else in my healing process.

I was unable to give my broken heart to him or anyone else. Under these circumstances, it would never have worked out between us. I had to let him go, and it wasn't easy. I felt horrible about it because he didn't deserve that. Although he knew that I was not over my ex, the heart can't control what it wants. Initially, I did tell him that I wasn't ready for a relationship but my actions said something completely different. Many believe that telling the person you don't want anything serious upfront will prevent them from developing feelings. This isn't always true. If you tell someone one thing but do another, nine times out of ten they will believe your actions over your words, especially if your actions are more aligned with what they want from you. I told my rebound that I didn't want a relationship, but my actions said, "Let's be monogamous," and those actions were more aligned with what he wanted, so he believed my actions over my words. When I finally snapped out of my rebound moment and wanted to slow down, it was too late and he had already fallen for me.

Now, this situation won't always be the case when it comes to rebounds. I have seen friends end up in extremely toxic relationships because they tried the Band-Aid approach and rebounded too quickly instead of dealing with the negative emotions of their past. The point I am attempting to prove is that you can't make conscious decisions about what to do with your heart when you're still emotionally burdened. Do not end up in an even worse scenario because you are too impatient to take the proper steps to heal. In my case, I could not assess the situation logically because I was trapped in my feelings. If I was not emotional, I would have known that it is a bad idea to date someone before you're over someone else, because you'll never be able to give your all. I didn't even stop to think that maybe I was caught in a rebound relationship. Since I don't want you to make the same mistake I did, let's look into some warning signs that your new boo may be a rebound.

REBOUND CHARACTERISTICS

- *They are not your typical type.* When you have a clear head and heart, you normally know exactly what you want in a mate. After coming out of a breakup, that vision often gets a little blurry. If you find yourself dating someone you wouldn't date if you weren't heartbroken, then most likely this is a rebound. If your normal preference is tall, dark, and handsome with a Bachelor's degree but your current guy is short and stumpy with only a high school diploma, then you may want to stop and reevaluate the situation. This is a sign that you just need someone to date no matter who it is, and that isn't good. Dating outside of the box is fine when you aren't relaxing your standards, but when you begin to go for less than what you originally felt you deserve, then you may be settling into a rebound situation.

- *You move really fast.* You met this person one week ago and you're already planning to bring them to the family barbeque. When you move this quickly, it's because you are trying to pick up where you and your ex left off. Instead of getting over your ex, you're subconsciously attempting to replace them with a new body because you don't want to start over. Do you even know this person? When was their first heartbreak? What type of relationship did they have with their grandparents? What gets them so annoyed that they completely shut down and no longer want to talk? These are questions you don't get answers to after knowing someone a week, these are things you learn about someone after you put time in. If you can't answer these questions yet but are thinking about moving them in, you are moving too fast and you need to pump your brakes

- ***You had sex immediately and it was good.*** Most people think sex can heal emotional wounds, so they use sex as an emotional outlet. The issue with this is sex can intensify emotions with the wrong person if you jump in bed too soon. If you are already emotionally unstable and someone comes into your life and offers great sex, you will become blinded by lust and will actually think this person is good for you because of how great the sex makes you feel. Don't start a meaningless relationship because sex blinded your better judgment. Do yourself a favor and stay far away from sex after a breakup.

- ***You have no direction for the relationship.*** Have

you ever dated someone that you couldn't see yourself with in the future? It wasn't that you didn't want a serious relationship, but you just didn't think of it with them. This is a strong sign that you're dating on the rebound. When you date just to feel better, you don't consider your future because you're just focused on feeling better. You could always see your prior relationships becoming serious, but now you just don't know or care. This is reckless dating, and you're better off spending time alone.

- *You randomly talk about your ex.* If you find yourself unknowingly speaking about your ex to this new person, then you are definitely dating a rebound. If you were over your ex, you would never risk ruining a new relationship by constantly bringing him or her up in conversation. If you are unsure if you're mentioning your ex up a lot, just ask the one you're dating now, "Do you think I talk about my past too much?" If their answer is yes, then you need time to cope.

- *You entertain everyone.* When dating a rebound, your options are open. That person may be a good catch, but you don't care because you yearn for attention. If you find yourself seeking other suitors you think may be better than your current situation, then you are most likely dating a rebound.

If more than three of these characteristics describe your current relationship, then you're in a rebound relationship and you may need to end it. Even if you have been with this person for over a year, it is still a rebound relationship. That is why you have had so much turmoil, because you were never supposed to be with this person in the first place. Do not let the fear of being lonely keep you stuck in a dead-end relationship. We will discuss loneliness in a later chapter.

For those of you in rebound relationships, you should terminate them immediately. You may think feeling better is easier than dealing with the pain of getting over your ex by yourself, but it isn't. You are actually just prolonging your healing process. Remove that emotional Band-Aid and start applying pressure, because that is where true healing begins.

The reason most of us seek rebounds is because it

distracts us from painful emotions. Rebounds are harmful distractions and should be avoided. Seek out healthy distractions instead. These can include hobbies, hanging out with close friends, and even working. I know it sounds extremely cliché, but it really works. It gets your mind off of the negative and helps you forget what you're really going through without involving another party. Yes, you'll likely slip and think about your ex and how you miss them, but the more you involve yourself in healthy distractions, the less you'll be reminded of what happened.

My healthy distraction was talking on the phone, watching a lot of Netflix, and exercising. When it came to talking on the phone, I would call or text everyone to avoid thinking about my situation. When watching Netflix, I would try to pick encouraging or comedic movies to make me laugh. Please don't watch emotionally draining movies like *The Notebook*, because you're bound to relapse and end up at your ex's door. Lastly, I began to exercise more. I honestly despise working out, but it is quite soothing when dealing with emotional stress. Even if it's just going for a long walk with your headphones on, it helps tremendously. If you are really angry, you can try kickboxing or cycling to relieve even more stress. The more rigorous the activity, the more emotional stress is released.

This phase is very difficult because the wound is still fresh and painful. You will most likely still cry randomly or get angry, but that's okay. This is a very uncomfortable stage, so expect to be stretched out of your comfort zone. Self-control and discipline will become your best friends. It will take time to get used to, but trust me, it will work. I am not looking to give you a temporary fix to your situation; I want you to be permanently healed. Follow these steps and you will emerge as a stronger individual. Remember, rebounds are only good in basketball.

"If the past is not resolved, future relationships will suffer. Let your heart heal before you open the door to another."
- Leon Brown

PHASE 4

The Closure Trap

I sought the formal definition of the word *closure* as it relates to a relationship, and the closest I found came from Merriam-Webster:

> **closure** – *a sense of resolution or conclusion at the end of an artistic work.*

After reading this definition, I made the assumption that when someone searches for closure to a relationship, they are referring to a conclusion or resolution. Although closure was originally meant to conclude an artistic work, somehow society has adjusted it to include resolution of disastrous situations and relationships.

Nowadays, there is a false belief that in order to heal properly from a relationship you need closure from your ex. But why do you need to conclude something that you already know is over? If you ask me, I think the word *closure* is nothing but an excuse, a justification to keep you wishing and hoping that a relationship that has already been concluded can somehow recommence. It is an excuse to go back into a toxic situation hoping to get a changed response or action you didn't get initially. It is an excuse to do the exact opposite of what the word closure really means, and that is keeping a door open that should be closed...and locked!

When you seek closure, you really aren't looking to close a chapter, you're simply searching for a result different from the one you received originally. Reality tells you, "No, this *can* never and *will* never work," but you just can't fathom the truth, so you must chase "closure" to conclude what has already been concluded. Simply put, it sounds outrageous when you say you need closure from a relationship that has already ended.

This word really hits home for me because I wasted

two years of my life trying to find closure from a situation that was over. I was nestled in the closure trap so deeply that no one could get me out. My friends tried to tell me, my intuition constantly warned me, and even my ex himself told me in so many words, but I didn't want to listen. My closure, or should I say closure-less, story began my junior year in college.

During my third year at Georgia State University, I got the opportunity to do an awesome internship in Orlando, Florida. The internship would run for about five months, and I was so excited. During my first weekend there, I attended a pool party. The party was cool, but I was a little standoffish because I didn't know anyone. While walking around amidst all those unfamiliar faces, I spotted a face I definitely wanted to see more of. There he stood, 6'4", light skin tone, low-cut hair, with major dimples. We locked eyes, and I just knew he would be my Orlando bae. The entire party, we kept our eyes locked on one another. I even gave him the little "I'm-interested-come-talk-to-me" grin. Maybe my grin was off that day, because we left the party without meeting. Two hours of distant flirting with nothing to show for it. I felt bummed, but since I'd only been in town a few days, I felt confident that I'd see him again.

The weekend went by quickly, and now it was time for orientation. As I waited in line to be checked in, my head was down as I looked through the orientation packet that had been given to me. Someone stood next to me and I turned to my left to see who it was. Lo and behold, it was the cutie from the pool party. Shocked, I did a double take, then shook my head and laughed. I guess he caught my reaction because he tilted his head and asked, "Weren't you at the pool party on Saturday?" I blushed, remembering how we'd studied each other at the party. We talked a little and exchanged numbers before orientation began. Little did I know; this was the beginning of a love affair I would never forget.

If you haven't noticed yet, I like to refer to my exes by their location so I will call him Orlando. After a while, Orlando and I became inseparable. We saw each other every single day, and the chemistry was undeniable. I introduced him to all of my friends I had made during the internship, and he brought me around his friends as well. We were a known couple and I would frequently get side eyes from jealous women who wanted my fine piece of man candy. Now he was fine, but the way he supported me was why I fell for him.

Orlando made me feel beautiful at a time when I struggled with my confidence. Before I moved to Florida to intern, I decided to do the big chop. I cut off all of my hair and had a baby Afro. I didn't know how to treat this new hair of mine. I had no idea what products to use or how to do a twist out on such short hair. This was way before the natural hair movement went into effect and before YouTube had all the natural hair gurus posting videos about how to style your hair. I did not feel pretty at all, but Orlando disagreed. He constantly reminded me that I was beautiful and that he wouldn't change anything about me. Even on my bad hair days, which occurred quite often because I was clueless about this hair, he would still compliment me and sometimes make suggestions on what I should do with my natural hair. He said it was beautiful and I just needed to get used to it. At a time when I struggled with self-love, he was my support system. I was used to men only seeing me all dolled up and glamorous but this was a man who found beauty in me when I thought I was at my ugliest.

A couple of months into the relationship, we both shared the 'L' word. I was so in love with this man, and at that point I felt we should start thinking about our relationship after the internship ended. I lived in Atlanta, Georgia and he lived in Columbus, Ohio. I felt that at the rate we were going, we could definitely do a long-distance relationship. He agreed, but also said we should just enjoy each other while in Florida and work the rest out later. That was the first red flag.

By the last month of our internship, Orlando and I were still closer than ever. We tried to spend every moment we could with each other because we knew the program was coming to an end. We took professional photos and bought each other keepsakes. I also kept one of his jacket, and we had a song we would sing to each other. Our time together was ending, and we were both very emotional about it. We both cried on our last day, but we promised to communicate daily to keep what we had going. Once we said our goodbyes, that was the beginning to the end for us.

I called and texted him when I returned to Atlanta,

but my calls were unanswered and I seldom received text responses. This went on for about a month, at which point I decided to just leave him alone, because obviously what we had wasn't as real as I believed it to be. He had spoken about forever before we parted, but I guess forever ended when we no longer lived in the same city.

Although I missed him, I began to put him in the back of my mind because I felt it was time to move on. Well, like most of my other exes, an alert seemed to go off in his head that I was moving on. I personally believe all exes with ill intentions instinctively know when you're doing well without them, and that their egos convince them to send mixed signals in order to cause confusion and doubt. That is precisely what Orlando did. Almost a year after our time together in Florida, he called me and apologized. He said he was confused because he had a situation back home and he didn't know who to choose. By situation, he meant he had a woman back in Ohio that he was dating the entire time he was involved with me in Florida. In retrospect, I guess it had just ended with her and he decided to call the woman next up, specifically me. Well, I naively accepted his apology and we started talking again. After learning of this secret woman, the last thing I should have done was accepted an apology. But I was young and still in love, holding on to that false hope I mentioned earlier. We talked daily for about two weeks, and then he did the disappearing act again. I then picked up the pieces of my heart and started my healing process over.

I had almost forgotten about Orlando after dating a few guys, but his "She's getting over me" alarm must've gone off because one year after the last disappearing act, he started reaching out once more. This time he brought out the big guns. He apologized again, then explained he'd been scared to date me because he knew we were soulmates. He even started tweeting that he found his soulmate and that he wouldn't let her get away and blah, blah, blah. I fell for it yet again, and when I told my friends they were concerned. When they asked why I would even let him back into my life, I said, "Well, I just really need closure." Oh, what a silly little rabbit I was. This time, I told Orlando that I needed to see him to assure that this was real. I needed to know that he wanted me as much as I wanted him, and the only way to get that sort of "closure" was to fly up to see him. So I did just that. I planned a trip to Columbus, Ohio because I wasn't going to take no for an answer.

The day came for my trip, and when I pulled in his driveway my palms were sweating. I hadn't seen this man in over two years. *"Will we still have chemistry? Will he still find me attractive? Are we starting something new? Is this really the end?"* All these questions went through my head, but I failed to think *"Why am I here?"*

Why did I need to closure from something that was obviously over when I left Florida two years before? This man disappeared on me twice, and that wasn't *closure* enough for me. He didn't even offer to meet my plane; I had to rent a car, and that wasn't closure enough for me. I traveled all the way to Ohio just to confirm what I already knew, that we were over. If he wanted me, we never would have lost touch to begin with. He never would have chosen to let me out of his life. I was so attached to the man who helped me find confidence when I felt I was my most unattractive that I couldn't see the man he truly was. He never wanted forever with me, he only wanted Florida. Yes, we had a great thing going during the internship, but he'd always known it would go no further. He'd even dropped hints when I tried to talk about our future together. So why did I feel I needed closure? Because I didn't want to believe the reality of the situation. His actions said we were over in Florida, but I thought that maybe his seeing me again would alter the reality of the situation. Needing closure was only an excuse for me to see him and attempt to rekindle a flame that had burned out when we left Florida. I had resolved and concluded that situation a long time ago.

Although I had closure all along, the trip wasn't totally in vain. It helped me to see the person he really was, and that he was not the guy I met in Florida. I don't know if the real Orlando was the man I saw when I flew to Ohio or the man I fell in love with in Florida, but they were indeed two different people. This Ohio fellow was an attention-seeker. All he cared about was being the center of attention. He was a party promoter part time, and when he took me to the club he promoted, he just left me to go tend to his business. I was entertained by some random nice guy who talked to me all night at the bar. This Ohio fellow was also disrespectful. I can recall us being in the mall together and some random thot walking by and him distancing himself from me so the thot would think he was alone. For those who don't know, a thot is an acronym for "that ho over there." I just laughed and walked the other way and let him speak to the thot. Going there revealed a side of him that needed to be seen so I could let go of forever. But did I really need to see something that was written in big bold red letters the entire time?

Being in the closure trap forces you to ignore reality because you want your fantasy to be true. I wasted money on a plane ticket, a rental car, new hair, nails, clothes, and most of all time just to find out something I already knew. We were over. If you want to waste time, energy, and money to get closure, then go right ahead. But before doing it, ask yourself, "What is getting closure from this going to conclude or resolve?" If you can't answer that logically, you may be stuck in the closure trap. Pay attention to the signs in front of you. You already have closure, but you may just be looking for an excuse to recommence.

"You have to accept that some chapters in our lives have to close without closure. There's no point in losing yourself trying to fix what's meant to stay broken."

\- Steve Maraboli

Give it to Your God

When it comes to religion, I know it can be a very tricky subject. Not everyone believes in the same thing, but I can guarantee you that you'll need some sort of spiritual guidance to release emotional ties from someone. I was baptized in 2014 and it changed my life. I stopped trying to have complete control over my life and started giving it to God. Prayer became a part of my life, and I looked to my Father in heaven to guide my decision-making. Before I was saved, I would have never gone to God about a man. I honestly felt that God was too busy saving souls and working with more important issues to help me through a breakup. Well, I was wrong. In most breakups we are afraid to walk away due to the fear that we are losing something and we won't be able to get it back if we leave. Most people wish they had a crystal ball and could look into the future to confirm whether or not they are doing the right thing. Guess what…God is like that crystal ball. He will not lead you astray, but you have to ask for His guidance first. I can recall an incident where He took my hand and guided me out of an unhealthy situation.

I dated a man in uniform once. I was really attracted to him, and our chemistry was off the charts. In retrospect, I believe that it was more sexual chemistry than anything, but that's a story for another day. We had been seeing each other for a couple of months and things were getting pretty serious. One day all that changed when baby mama drama surfaced.

On this day, I called him and told him I was going to stop by his job and say hi before I went into work. He said okay and to just text him when I was on my way. I headed to his job and sent a text informing him that I'd be there shortly. I had visited his job several times before at different points during the day and had met several of his co-workers. I visited him enough times to become familiar with which car belonged to which co-worker. Well on this particular evening, something wasn't right because there was an unknown car in the parking lot. Usually when I would visit him at his job, he always comes out of the building and meets me before I pull into the parking lot. That day, I was already in the parking lot and he was taking an unusual amount of time to come out of the building. Although my intuition told me something was shady, I told myself to relax. While I was waiting for him, I saw a woman come out of his job and that was very odd because there were no women scheduled on his shift and she looked like the mother of his child. I knew her face from a few pictures I'd seen on Facebook. I found her profile after she commented under a picture of his daughter. Don't judge me, I am sure most women comment creep to make sure there's nothing fishy going on.

Of course I wasn't upset when I saw her because I knew they had a child together and they would have to speak for the child's wellbeing. My only concern was the fact that he didn't mention she would be stopping by. I continued to wait in the car patiently, and finally he emerged from the building…after the mother of his child had left the parking lot. When he came to my car, I mentioned that I'd seen a young lady leaving and asked if he knew who she was. He said she was a guest and he had given her a tour of his workplace. Although he worked for the city and people asked for tours all the time so it wasn't uncommon that he would give a tour, I knew he was lying. I was about to leave, so I leaned in to give him a hug and a kiss before getting back into my car. Suddenly, the "guest" he had allegedly just given a tour drove back into the parking lot, slamming on her brakes when she saw us. She rolled her window down and yelled, *"Really?!"* He went toward her car, but she pulled off before he reached her. I asked him what that was all about, at which time he told me the truth. He said she was the mother of his child and she stopped by to give him some paperwork about their daughter. I was upset because he had lied to me. I got in my car and drove off, still fuming.

I got to work with this incident still on my mind, so I decided to text him.

You didn't have to lie to me. I knew the entire time who she was, but you created this ridiculous story about you giving someone a tour of your workplace. I know you have kids and I know those kids have mothers. Your not telling me the truth says you have something to lie about, which means you have something to hide.

All he could say was.

We will discuss this face to face tomorrow. Have a good night at work.

Well, the next day came and I didn't hear from him. I was LIVID. I texted and called and he didn't reply until 11PM that night. He said his uncle had passed away and he had been with his family all day. I felt bad but I was still angry. Being the thoughtful person that I am, I told myself I would put my anger aside and try to console him through his loss. I decided to buy him a feel-better cake and deliver it to let him know that even though I was still upset, I did care about him.

Well, it didn't quite work out the way I planned. When I arrived with the cake, I tried to disguise my irritation with a smile. I was still upset about the baby mama incident because we hadn't discussed it. I am horrible at hiding my emotions, so he picked up on the tension immediately.

Note to self: *Never try to force yourself to be okay with something you know you're angry about. Give yourself time to feel better before attempting to reach out to that person, no matter what he or she is going through. You must make sure you take care of yourself first.*

We got into an argument and I told him how I felt. He made the excuse that he didn't lie, that his daughter's mother actually *was* a guest and he'd shown her around. Say what now? He really stood there with a straight face and boldly spewed this ridiculous lie? I wasn't buying it, and I stood my ground. Well, so did he. Nothing was solved that day. My petty side told me to grab the cake and shove it in his face, but my logic wouldn't let me do that. I just left, still mad and with nothing resolved.

After I slept on it, I felt bad for even arguing with him since his uncle had passed away. I thought about just being the bigger person and being patient with him to put the incident behind us. I thought about letting all of it go and just moving on and giving him a second chance. I felt it was time to ask God for the answer, so I prayed. Well, He was quick with His response, because as soon as I was done praying I turned up the radio and a gospel song just happened to be playing. The crazy thing was that I wasn't listening to a gospel station. The song playing was *Live Through It* by James Fortune. The song mentions not to beg anyone to remain in your life, just let go. Hearing this confirmed for me that it would be useless to try to save our relationship—or should I say "situationship." After that day I was done. But in retrospect, if I'd prayed in the beginning then none of this would've happened.

Let's take prayer a step forward. What if I prayed in the very beginning asking God if I should pursue a relationship with this man in the first place? Yes, he was attractive and he saved lives for a living, but was he right for me?

Back then, I didn't pray when I met a man because I felt that it was too soon and unnecessary, but I now realize the need to pray at every moment of my decision-making, especially in the beginning. He was never right for me and I would've known that if I prayed about him first. God gives us signs when we don't even ask for them; we just have to pay attention. I was thankful that I was able to see the kind of person he was by his handling of the baby mama quarrel. I was also grateful for my discipline and ability to walk away when I heard God say do so. Don't ignore the signs when He says leave; He is revealing this stuff for a reason. It isn't always the devil trying to mess up what you have because he doesn't want to see you happy. Many times it is God trying to reveal to you that you are in an unhealthy situation and you need to get out because He has something better. Trust God and let Him work in your life.

Praying, for me, is not just seeking signs from God. I also pray because I need God to help me through those tough emotional days. When you're going through heartbreak, there will be days when you feel empty and like you're all alone. This is when you must let go and let

God. This means that you have to let go of the worry, the anger, the sadness, the guilt, the regret and all the pain in order to let God heal you from within. All you have to do is pray and have faith that He will heal your heart and you will be just fine.

If you are not one who prays, give it to your God however you know how. Confess, chant, or meditate, but you have to understand that you can't heal alone. You can even give it to the universe if that makes you happy. Bringing good vibes into your life and your spirit can and will uplift you. Trust the process and give it to your God.

Psalm 73:26

My flesh and my heart may fail, but God is the strength of my heart and my portion forever.

PHASE 6

Perception is Reality

When you initially get your heart broken, a huge part of the pain is the false belief that no one will compare to your ex. You think about how attractive they were, how muscular he was, and how her butt was so big. You think about how well they treated you, how she cooked your meals, and how he always surprised you with date nights. You think about how good the sex was, how he knew what spots to touch, and how she always wore sexy lingerie. I get it; you miss them. But in order to jump this hurdle and get to the finish line you need to retrain your brain to think differently about them. I'm sure you've heard the saying, 'perception is reality'. Keep that phrase in mind, because how you perceive your ex after the breakup will reflect the length of time it takes you to move on. I'm going to help you perceive them the right way so you can speed up this process.

TIP 1: THINK ABOUT THE BAD

Okay, I know this may sound crazy because you need to remain positive, but when you think of your ex I need you to get real negative. Going through a breakup causes you to remember all the good things Jane or John did, which in turn only makes you feel worse. I'd like you to think instead about the things they did that got on your nerves. Think about the way he snored like a gorilla, or the clumps of hair she left in the sink. This will allow you to stay strong when you think about contacting them or driving to their house to stand outside their window singing Sam Smith *Stay with Me*.

In the past when I wanted to call my ex or look at his Instagram it was because I was remembering everything about him that made me smile. To counter that, I began to think about the bad things and the reason why I left in the first place. If you can't remember the bad, then grab that letter to your ex I told you to write, and read it. You need to return to the time when you realized that your leaving them or them leaving you was for the best.

TIP 2: NOT EVERYONE YOU LOSE IS A LOSS

I'm sure everyone has heard the song *Best thing I Never Had* by Beyoncé, but if you haven't, go listen to it and let it marinate. In the song she speaks about how she wanted someone so bad at one point, but after all was said and done, he became the best thing she never had. It's kind of like that old crush you had in high school that you were crazy about, but when you saw them last month in the mall your first thought was, "What was I *thinking*?!" Think about your ex that way. Of course they have some good traits, but were those traits really meant for you? When I think about the men I've dated who were great catches but the relationships failed, I consider that the reason it didn't work out was probably because we weren't really that compatible. When I say everyone isn't a loss it doesn't necessarily mean that the person was bad, but possibly just that the two of you were incompatible. You need to embrace this freedom so you can find someone you're more compatible with. So stop perceiving your failed relationship as a loss and recognize that it was really a gain.

TIP 3: THERE IS BETTER OUT THERE

It is so hard to see the silver lining sometimes when going through a breakup…especially when you were so in love with this person you thought was just perfect. Well, I am here to tell you that no man or woman is perfect and that there will always be better. Now, when you're in a relationship, it's great when you think about your boo as irreplaceable because you love them so much, but truth be told, no one is actually irreplaceable. You had a great run, but it's time to pass the baton to someone else. I say this because so many people get caught up with the thought that they cannot find anyone better when this is just false. You must understand that everything happens for a reason in life, and if someone leaves your life for whatever reason, it may well be because something better awaits you.

TIP 4: REDISCOVER THE TRUE YOU

One of the biggest reasons people tend to remain in an

unhealthy relationship is because they have completely lost themselves. They forget how to function without having that person with them, as if they have no identity without them. Well, this could be because you have compromised and sacrificed so much for your relationship that you don't even remember who you are anymore. In a healthy relationship, you know exactly who you are separate from your partner, because your partner encourages you to stay true to who you are and accepts all parts of you. When you have someone who is constantly nagging you about the things you do and how you act, encouraging you to change facets of your personality, then that isn't healthy. They don't love you for you, because if they did they wouldn't ask you to change so much of who you are. True acceptance in a relationship is your partner seeing you for exactly who you are and appreciating all of it, good and bad, and not nagging you to change. Take this breakup as a sign that you need to figure out who you are again, because maybe you lost yourself, and a large component of your current pain is your inability to see who you are without them.

TIP 5: YOU ARE WORTHY OF MORE

We have all made mistakes and we all have flaws, but don't let that keep you stuck in an unhealthy relationship. I've seen women remain with abusive boyfriends because that man has convinced them that they have gained too much weight or they have kids now so no one will ever want them. These are all lies engineered to keep you under their control because they don't want to see you happy. There is someone for everyone, so don't think that having imperfections or baggage means you have to settle for less. Men, this goes for you, too. Maybe you lost your job or you don't have money to splurge. There is still a good woman out there ready and willing to love you for the good in your heart. Don't let your insecurities keep you from believing that you don't deserve the best. We are all worthy of a strong, unconditional love, so never settle for less. You are worthy of the best!

"Sometimes good things fall apart so better things can fall together."

\- Marilyn Monroe

PHASE 7

Fighting Lonely

There will come a time when you get past the crying, past the constant thoughts, and past the flat out anger. You will feel at ease and begin to see that everything will be all right. This sounds great, right? Not really. This stage is by far your most vulnerable point, so proceed with caution. I know you're confused because I just said that you are no longer crying or wishing that your ex would get abducted by aliens and be tortured to death, so why am I telling you to proceed with caution? Because this is the stage where my good friend, loneliness, likes to kick in. If you didn't know, loneliness is a complex and usually unpleasant emotional response to isolation or lack of companionship. The lack of companionship is the part that affects your psyche the most. When you're so accustomed to having someone of the opposite sex around to satisfy your companionship needs, you begin to miss that feeling, which leaves you lonely and vulnerable… very dangerous for the healing process.

How is it dangerous, you ask? Well, when one is lonely, they stop thinking logically and begin to think emotionally and lead with their heart. What's so tricky about this is half the time you don't even know you're doing it. Have you ever had thoughts of reaching out to that person you were talking to before you chose your ex because they now seem very appealing? You're lonely. Or have you looked at that person's Facebook page that always makes nice comments and started to think things like, "Well, they're not that bad, maybe I'll go out with them"? You're lonely. These small things seem innocent and harmless, but they're not. You start to think your decisions are logical and not being led by the recent emotional effects of your breakup. Well, I am here to tell you that you are absolutely wrong and that step you're about to take will only set you back in the process. You are just trying to fill that lonely void. Stop! Do *not* interrupt your healing process for a quick fix, because—trust me—it's not worth it.

I had a situation where, out of nowhere, I was dumped by a guy I really liked. I was so hurt that I wasn't even mad, just sad and stuck in a *why?* frame of mind. I just knew it was a joke and he would come back and yell, *"Sike!"* Well, I was wrong about that; it was really over. After being dumped, I went through my normal proper healing measures. I deleted his number, I cried, I called upon my friends to help comfort me, I emotionally binged on snacks, and I tried to stay busy to keep my mind off my hurt. Well, after two months I stopped thinking about him all the time and started to feel at ease with his decision. Around this time, I reached out to one of my exes who stayed in New York. We hadn't seen each other in years, and I could admit that I missed him. It ended because he didn't want a long distance relationship. Of course, I hadn't wanted it to end, but I respected his decision and we remained distant friends.

Initially when I reached out, I just wanted to catch up and see how he was doing. Well, frequent texts turned into FaceTime calls, and FaceTime calls turned into him purchasing a plane ticket to Atlanta to come visit me. In my mind, this was merely an innocent trip for two friends to catch up… but in my heart this was a possible weekend for rekindling an old flame and filling that void I didn't even realize existed. I was in complete denial about what this visit really meant, but I was ready for whatever the weekend held.

When the weekend arrived, I was super excited. I groomed every part of my body, including waxing those unmentionable areas, just in case. I know you're thinking, who does this for just a friendly weekend? A person in complete and utter denial about what's really going on, that's who. Well, he arrived and our weekend began. Within the first two hours, we went from friends to friends with benefits, if you know what I mean. We kept it going for the entire weekend, acting like a couple in bed and out. He paid for everything, and if someone tried to flirt with me while we were out, I ignored them, even if I was attracted to them, and he did the same. During this time I honestly didn't know what it all meant. Was our relationship on again, or were we both just living in the moment? While I pondered this, I never actually asked him because I was too afraid of the answer. The biggest reason for my fear was because I couldn't take another emotional hit. I couldn't handle any more rejection from someone I cared about. I think God heard my plea to not be rejected, but He was more concerned with me seeing the bigger picture. So instead of me avoiding the truth, God decided to reveal it as clear as day.

We were at dinner and having a great time. We were reminiscing on some good times, and then, out of nowhere, he began talking about his love life.

"It's crazy dating in a big city. It just seems like everyone is super fake and has an ulterior motive. Man, I haven't had a real connection in so long. I really feel like giving up on dating, 'cause it just isn't working for me."

While listening to him speak, I just knew he was about to say something along the lines of, "Let's try again." I was blushing in anticipation as I waited for him to spit it out. And then he continued.

"There's this one chick back home I'm feeling, but I'm

not really sure how to approach her. We've been friends for a while, but I don't think she's feeling me like that. She gets me all nervous when I'm around her. What do you think I should do? Leave it alone or take a shot?"

You heard that? Yep, that was my face shattering onto the floor. Beads of embarrassment formed on my forehead, and all I could do was give him a nervous grin and a positive response.

"Go for it! You got this."

I sat there the rest of the dinner with my mind reeling with questions. *What does this chick have that I don't have? Why did he even come down here if he already has someone back home he's interested in? Why not me?* As all of those questions seeped in, it was then that I realized that his coming was a mistake.

The reason it was a mistake wasn't because he didn't want me, it was because I *wanted* him to want me. My lonely brain was lying to myself the entire time. I had convinced myself that this was just an innocent weekend when the entire time I really wanted companionship. I told myself that even if we crossed the line, I would be okay because I knew we were just friends. My lonely brain didn't account for how emotionally weak I was from just getting out of a relationship. It also didn't consider that being rejected again would be a hit to my already low self-esteem after recently being dumped. My lonely brain had only one thing on its mind, and that was to be under a man because I was yearning companionship.

In moments of loneliness, you have to be careful not to think with your heart or let your emotions lead. If you need help figuring out if you're thinking emotionally rather than logically, ask your best friend. That best friend you don't want to call when you're doing something dumb because you know they're going to make you shut it down. It doesn't always have to be a friend. It could be a parent, a mentor, or even a complete stranger. The goal is to not consult with yourself, because your loneliness will lead you to make a rash decision.

This not only goes for individuals from your past, it goes for new individuals who may enter your life as well. You have to stop and ask yourself, "Am I really ready for something new?" I know we've already talked about rebounds, but this is the stage where you need to be aware of catching that rebound the most. Oh, and remember when I said to think about the bad? You'd better think hard, because this is also the stage where that ex you're trying to move past starts to seem not so bad. You'll start to use "yeah, but" statements. What are "yeah, but" statements? "Well, yeah, he forgot my birthday and didn't show up to the birthday dinner when Grandma Brenda was dying to meet him, but he got me the new iPhone for Christmas." Or "Yeah, she slept with two of my best friends *and* my cousin, but she paid my car note every month." You get the point, right? At this stage you feel settled in your emotions, so you think you're strong enough to be around your ex or that new cutie who approached you in the Wendy's line, but unfortunately you are not. I know you feel 100% ready and you hate that awful feeling of lonely, but you'll feel even better and stronger once you get past lonely. You have to keep doing those healthy distractions we discussed in previous chapters, because the last thing you want to do is go backward. Getting past lonely is an extremely hard task, but it can definitely be done. The main task is to not interrupt the process.

> *"At the innermost core of all loneliness is a deep and powerful yearning for union with one's lost self."*
>
> - Brendan Francis

PHASE 8

Self-Reflection

I like to think of myself as fine wine, getting better with time. Through adversity, I was able to come out stronger and better by looking at each breakup as a lesson as opposed to a struggle. If you're so caught up on how hurt you are instead of what this situation has taught you, you will get nowhere. I believe everything happens for a reason, and most cases you can identify that reason by self-reflection. To me, retrospect is the best view because it allows you to place your current self in a past situation and see where you went wrong. You can then store that knowledge so you won't make that same mistake again.

Throughout my life, I was always labeled as the

outspoken friend. You know the one, she's super bubbly and gets along with everyone...but don't piss her off because she will snap. Yes, that's me. I love everyone, but I don't have a problem standing up for myself. When people see individuals like me, they perceive us as strong. They think our not being scared to "pop off" gives us strength. Well, this is not always true. Strength is not measured by how loud you can yell or how many fights you can win. It is measured by your endurance, your ability to get knocked down repeatedly, both mentally and emotionally, and still have the strength to get back up. Don't get me wrong, I am a *very* strong person. But my strength isn't due to my being willing to slap someone if need be, it's due to my having been knocked down by love multiple times and still have the ability to get back up again. It wasn't until I really looked at my life in retrospect that I realized how strong I really am. Every time I went through a heartbreak, I would always say to myself, "This is the one, I am going to snap and do the unthinkable," but the unthinkable never happened. Every person who broke my heart walked away without me doing the unexpected violent girl routine or trying to ruin their life like that woman in the movie *Fatal Attraction*. My strength allowed me to walk away without needing to get payback. The best revenge is living well, right?

Knowing your strength allows you to push yourself past your comfort zone. The reason so many people can't move on is because they haven't recognized their strength and they feel they're too weak to move on. Guess what? You have the strength to do anything you want to do. Never underestimate your strength, because everyone is strong in their own way. Anyone can move on, because moving on is up to you. It's something you have control over, and you are strong enough to do it! Everyone has strengths, and it's up to you to recognize them and put them into play.

I have a friend who was going through a situation with a guy. That fool really put her through it. She gave him money, paid for his hotel rooms, and even gave that fool's mother money when he wasn't able to. I know I am using fool excessively, but I need you to understand how much of a fool that fool was. After an entire year of this so-called courtship, she finally realized that he was never going to be with her. This was a hard pill to swallow after doing so much for that fool. Yes, she went about this situation the wrong way. She should've never courted a man but instead allowed a man to court *her*. That's really neither here nor there. The part that shocked me the most was that after all this, she didn't cause bodily harm to him. If it were me, I probably would have run him over with my car and told the insurance company I hit a deer so I could get back some of that money I spent on him. Her ability to walk away after being used proved her strength. It's easy to key a car or slice some tires, but it's hard to just walk away. I myself am very emotional, and when I'm wronged my inner strength wavers and I tend to blow up. No, I have never physically attacked a guy or damaged any of his belongings, but I definitely let him feel the wrath of my words. For this reason, I had to give it to my friend; she is definitely stronger than me in that aspect.

The crazy part about this is that she didn't even recognize her strength. She felt weak and used. I understood that, given the situation, but the fact that she hadn't gone off on him should have made her feel strong and unbreakable. She would say things like, "I wish I could handle things like you do," and I hated when she did that, because she was critically comparing her strengths to mine, not understanding that my lack of self-control made *me* the weak one. I had to point out to her how her behavior actually made her strong.

By letting go and just walking away she had demonstrated forgiveness. This is a tough muscle to build, and many people wish they had it. People who forgive are happier because they don't retain emotional baggage.

Her ability to have that fool's back in his time of need made her dependable. She showed this trait to the wrong person, but dependability is a great strength, and her next man will be lucky that she has it.

Waiting a year for him to get his act together showed patience. Again, she showed this to the wrong man, but this is still a strength.

Finally, her ability to snap back from being emotionally and financially abused by this man proved that she's resilient. She didn't ask him for any of the money back. She just knew she would be okay without getting anything from him.

All these strengths from a person who tried to convince me she was weak.

What are *your* strengths? What are the positive things you've brought to your relationships? What about the strengths you showed when you walked away? If you don't know what makes you strong, then this is your time to figure it out. Self-reflecting is looking back on that relationship and figuring out what you brought to the table. Once you figure it out, write it down. This is a confidence-building action that will help you understand that you didn't lose them, but *they* lost *you*. If you're having trouble identifying those strengths, ask your parents or close friends who know you. They'll give you a list of strengths you probably never even thought about.

Self-reflection is a wonderful way to learn as well as boost your confidence, but you must reflect on the correct things. This is not a time to reflect on where the relationship went wrong so you can attempt to fix it. This is a time for self, a time to focus on you and only you. You are figuring out what signs you may have missed or what you wanted out of the relationship that you didn't receive. You need to know all this so you don't make the same mistakes in your next relationship. You are also focusing on your strengths so you know your worth going out into the dating scene. After successfully completing this phase, you'll be able to clearly see the lessons from your past and how reflecting can be a blessing to your future. You have made it through, and you are so close to X'ing your ex.

"A break up is like a broken mirror. It is better to leave it alone than hurt yourself trying to fix it."

\- Linda Randall Wisdom

Conclusion

Congratulations! You have made it to the end of the book. Unfortunately, this is only the beginning of your healing process. Reading this book is only half the battle. Applying these phases is the most important. Here are a few tips to help you apply these steps properly:

TIP 1

You will most likely have to read this book more than once. You do this because your first go-round was just a skim-through. Now you want to reread it and figure out precisely how it applies to your life. Make sure you have a highlighter handy as well to highlight those points that really stand out for you.

TIP 2

Be sure to take notes, especially on the phases you believe you will struggle with the most. This will help you commit these phases to memory so you can really X your ex this time.

TIP 3

Please follow directions. When I suggest writing something down, please do so because merely thinking it won't work. The more you commit to this process, the better the results will be.

TIP 4

Please don't rush this process. As I said in the beginning, everyone's journey will be different. Breakups occur on a case-by-case basis, so don't compare your process to anyone else's. Just remain strong and take your time with the phases. You *will* get through this.

TIP 5

Get accountability partners. Let your friends know what you're doing and ask them to hold you accountable.

I'm sure they'll be very glad to do so. This will help you when you are tempted to call your ex or when you weaken and consider going on a rebound date. Being held accountable will give you motivation, because when you don't follow through, you aren't just letting yourself down, but you're letting your friends down, too.

Applying these tips should give you a head start on what to do now that you're done reading. Also, do not beat yourself up if you fall short during a few phases. People make mistakes, but it's how you come back from those mistakes that counts. If you relapse during a phase, don't dwell on it. Get back on track and continue to the next phase. Remember your strength and keep pushing.

I hope this book has shed some light on your current situation. I also hope you feel empowered and confident that you can and will heal your heart. I wish you the best of luck on your journey toward X'ing your ex.

Made in the USA
Columbia, SC
05 July 2020